He Prepares a Table for Me Before My Enemies

h.e. newell

Copyright © 2021 (H.E. Newell).

All rights reserved. No part of this publication may be reproduced, distributed, or transmitted, in any form or by any means, including photocopying, recording, or other electronic or mechanical methods, without the prior written permission of the Author, except in the case of brief quotations embodied in critical reviews and certain other noncommercial uses permitted by copyright law. For permission requests, write to throneroomjewel@gmail.com

Any references to historical events, real people, or places are used fictitiously. Names, characters, and places are products of the author's imagination.

Book Layout © 2016 BookDesignTemplates.com

Tree of Life (TLV) Translation of the Bible. Copyright © 2015 by The Messianic Jewish Family Bible Society.

Dedication

To my beautiful mother, Paula. I'm so glad you partnered with Heaven to bring me into my destiny! I love you most!

And my sweet Geri mom. Your faith and love teach me something new every day.

For Michael, my darling, my soul friend. The greatest joy of my heart has been to seek the Face of the Lord with you.

King Jesus! Every moment with You is the most beautiful.

My Adonai! Thank You for answering my violent cries to see the Glory Realm.

Holy Spirit! May I always breathe in unity with You.

Psalm 23:5 (TLV)

You prepare a table before me in the presence of my enemies.

You have anointed my head with oil, my cup overflows

Contents

Dedication..3

Promises..6

Welcome..7

Poetry..13

Dark Sayings..45

Psalms..57

From an old Journal..81

Prophetic Words..119

About the Author..147

Blue agate sky,

citrine sunset,

smiling over new beginnings...

Every step

brings me closer

to the promises of God.

Welcome to the banquet!!!

I'm sharing the fruit of a life spent leaping into the things of God with both feet...with you.

At a very young age, I embraced the cost of a life spent on Jesus. I embraced the wooing in my spirit to walk out the life of a mystic. I do not regret a moment since.

Like an adventurer, I sought out the most valuable, well-hidden fruit there could possibly be. This sort of fruit costs everything. Retrieving it nearly killed me a few times, and often left me alone in the world. Sometimes the opposition and despair were so great, I wrestled myself to keep from giving up. I didn't ask questions most of the time; I just went deeper. Determined. Consumed by my glorious obsession. Fully addicted to the Glory of the Lord.

Most of the treasures in this book were received between 2002 and 2006. I was in such a deep time with the Lord, that I had a difficulty functioning in the natural.

I travelled through time and space with Jesus and angels, I saw my other self and prayed for his life, I visited nations and heard the cries of the land for deliverance, and I spent months at a time in visions and trances. It was a bittersweet time when I was hearing so specifically... the Voice of God. And yet, many of the people around me spoke religious judgement against me. It seemed the loudest voices couldn't accept that God would tell me anything. Somehow, they penetrated my soul more deeply than the voices who believed with me.

I wrote letters to the man I call my other self. I saw him, heard him, sat with him... I loved and prayed for a man I only saw in my spirit. When Jesus showed me all the details about this one, I was told that it couldn't possibly be God, He wouldn't tell me those things.

I spoke in dark sayings and parables when I prayed for people. Holy Spirit would give me pictures and riddles, such as the Candy Maker you will read about later. I was told that no one speaks in parables anymore, so it wasn't of God.

I wrote psalms of praise and imprecation, declarations of His love and action on our behalf. I was told that I, as a fiction writer, was just copying what I read in the Bible. No one writes psalms anymore, so it wasn't of God.

All of these statements meant that *I* was not of God! Then who was I? Who was this man He kept showing me? What spirit was I of?? Was everything a lie?

My mind was in torment. Chaotic, tumultuous attacks came against my family like stormtroopers. I was so afraid that I was still walking in the occult, I thought I deserved every calamity.

Looking back, the most heartbreaking part of this season was the lack of understanding of who our God is, how perpetual His nature is, and how confident "strong believers" were in this lack of understanding. So much of this was released over me, I doubted my sanity at times, and my soul was in such anguish, my body eventually shut down. I forgot everything... for several years, until the Lord healed my broken body and soul.

Yes, Jesus put me back together. He is redeeming every moment.

I am still scribing the story of my redemption. I am scribing the process, the beautiful journey I have walked with Jesus. He has rewritten my narrative, so that I see the banquet in the forefront. Where my focus was once directed at the battle, the attack, the struggle, all I can see is the celebration. I couldn't write about the journey until I could confidently see it through the lens of the victorious one rather than the struggling one. I couldn't invite you to the table until I could truly accept the invitation to my own banquet.

I am the guest of honor, you see. I am seated at His right hand, the oil of Gladness has been poured out over me, and my cup overflows with the sweetest wine. This banquet is all about me and my Bridegroom, all about our love for one another. It is His announcement to my enemy: "Look at my favourite one! Look how strong and victorious she is!" It is also His announcement to Heaven: "Look at this daughter of Zion! Look how she has taken her rightful seat here!" And presiding over this banquet in my honor, is the Great I AM. The One who knew I would assume my place before time was time.

I couldn't invite you to this banquet until I could see the beauty of it for myself. Every poem, every psalm, every vision... a delicacy. Like lamb cheeks or violet sweets. Every moment celebrates everything I have suffered or experienced. Celebrates every experience I have had in the spirit. All of it is spread out before me like exotic delicacies fit for, well, a queen.

Some of these delicacies might be too rich for you. Some might seem too simple. It's all valid. Holy Spirit knows we all have unique palates. We all taste things differently. That's why there's so much to choose from at a banquet. Our Host loves to give us luxury as He caters to every guest. We choose to taste and see that the Lord is good. Or not. Regardless of our choice, He is good.

He sets a table for me in the presence of my enemies. He never stops. He adds to the table daily.

Sometimes the enemy is a spirit. Sometimes the enemy is sitting beside you in a prayer meeting. Just know that when the Lord sets your table they aren't invited. In fact, they can only see the beautiful delicacies on fine linens and polished silver that came out of every victory. They can't savor the sweetness of anything.

This is my banquet. The table set for me in the presence of my enemies. Set by the Lover of my soul.

Everything you see before you here...came when my head was bloody but unbowed. I have transcribed journal entries, chat logs, and emails from this season. Sacred moments with the Lord. Hours of prophetic intercession and praise with the precious ones who believed with me, who will be at my banquet. Heartfelt moments where Jesus and my other self were equally real to me. I hope that you will be challenged to be real and desperate for God and the beauty of His presence.

I've left most of it in its rawest state, so you can relive the moments with me. I've left you spaces to draw, write, ponder...to dive in with me. Let us have a conversation about our worthy pursuit.

Your table will be a celebration of you. He is setting it for you in the presence of your enemies. He has the final say on the guest list. He is honoring you, loving you, presenting you as one He is so pleased with, and I can't wait to see it!

Let this be the year we assume our places beside our King!

Poetry

When My Hair is Silver
12 December 2005

When I am silver haired and tired,
an old lady living in quiet whispers,
I shall look on my life with deep, serene joy
recalling how sublime
even the darkest of days were.
Clothed in the peace of God,
which will have rested upon me completely,
I will feel beautiful at last.

Yet here in this moment...
Oh! this turbulent mind of mine!
Memories flood
like hostile, unkind waters raging
breaking the dam in my mind that holds them back.
Petulant things!
stirring up the still pool
stones
ripples

waves
distorting my reflection,
rising high and blocking the sunlight.
Fierce creatures!
I will starve them out!

In fact, I am in the brightest sun,
the fullest moon of my life these days.
Silver hair begins to peek through the chestnut,
my children just discovering themselves,
and I
like a child, finding me at last.

When the sun of my days begins to set,
the silver of my hair shimmering like
sweet soft strands of moonlight with me always,
I shall smile softly
recalling the victorious moments when I,
frightened yet determined,
weathered the storm
defeated Leviathan and set myself free.

My children grown
perhaps more will come to me by then,
I shall see the legacy all this living of mine has bought them.
I shall pull my shawl tightly around me,
my head resting on soft pillows,
and bless them one by one,
impart my spirit to them

as I lie in violet quilts
made once for my sweet love
when my hands were far nimbler and finer.

When I am leaving this world to see

the Beauty Realm forever
I shall rise above the clouds,
my spirit living eternally.
The children long passed receiving me
(Perhaps the one I quilted for also)
there with my Bridegroom waiting.

When I am an old lady
those moments will be close to me
and every moment that's passed
will be a thread in some lovely shawl my Lover
will cover me with
made beautiful by each lovely soul
I met along the journey.
Recalling even this moment
when I, with deep longing in my heart,
wrote these lines with tears in my eyes.

Hold me now, as I slip into
some beautiful peaceful rest,
here in crushed velvet covers.
Be with me as I dream
of you
of tomorrow

of my silver hair shimmering like so much silk
against your cheek.

11 October 2004
Speak to Me

Speak to me in
your quiet way,
your sweet peace
fills my head,
my spirit,
my senses.

Touch my heart,
rearrange me-
make me like you,
make me love,
lovely,
lovable...

you are love in me.

I would endure all
pains for you
even so small
in comparison
to
the selfless love you
have for me.
Make me selfless.
Make me a reflection
of you,
beautiful,

pure,
precious.

Do you see your

reflection when you look
at me with
all my flaws?
all my scars?
Will you polish me
and create something
worthwhile,
valuable,
useful?

I hear you now,
you say
I am
all I have asked.
I want to be more,
speak to me,
show me the way.

For my other self.
2 February 2004

search deep,
see the dawn
new days coming
like soft sweet kisses on
a baby's cheek
hear the days begin
with a song

.

the world opened up for
you and
I saw you step
out and taste it
like a berry picked
fresh for you.
was it sweet?
taste another,
there's a whole
garden waiting for you

.

I sang a song
in the night
you slept like an angel
softly breathing
peaceful
quiet dreaming
sleep well this night
when you wake the

20   h.e. newell

world will open for you
again

I give you a pearl
30 August 2004

beaded pillow
soft prayer shawl
linen night gown
quietly laying out
beneath the great masterpiece

I feel like Michelangelo
I reach up and touch
Him

the pearl in the midst
of the velvet...
I could take it for just a moment
and give it to you
He's given it to us
to share

my heart wanders
to another place... time...
my spirit is content there...
the same pearl,
perfect and beautiful,
looks down in gentle admiration
on you...
this pearl hears, sees, knows...
we've spoken
Him and I and this pearl...

He promised and you spoke,
you spoke and He promised
I rest in this
wooden boards begin to feel...
different against my back
my hands feel
earth beneath them
grass under my feet
beneath my head is...
I've felt it before many times
as I turn my head I see
a profile turning, smiling...

the city on the hill cannot be moved
I will go to it
and I will stretch out under the
great masterpiece
and this pearl
will smile...
because I dream no longer

I want to sing this all to you
23 August 2004

"who am I?" he asks...
as though he isn't amazing

"you." I smile

another day
he asks again
"who am I?"
all I can do is smile...

he has no idea...
I want to look deep
I want him to see what I see
when he smiles
laughs
works
sleeps
when he teaches me things
in his gentle wonderful way

how can he not know
who he is?
who I see?
who I love?
"who am I?"
he asks again...

"you are beautiful, remarkable!
you are..."

the most amazing thing,
the most radiant
way about him
is that he has no idea
all that my reply encompasses...
when all I can do
is smile and whisper
"you"

The Sun and the Rain
2004

I recall the rain
falling softly on my face
as I stood out under the stars
the wind blowing with such
determination, my hair dancing with it
and the clouds trying
to keep away the light of the moon...

can light be kept out?

and you...
I recall your voice in my ear
as you shared the sun
warm and golden like Samson's honey
I can still picture it
kissing your sweet face and
smiling on you as only He would

you shared your light with me
like some alabaster box
with precious oils in it
a perfect gift that only He could know

perhaps you understood
how those moments reached deep
light and dark
sun and moon

he and she
you and me
and the peace that planted itself in me then
joy unspeakable
as though only He stood between us
balancing...
His own joy complete

all I can do is cast my gaze down
smiling
recalling it all
peace wrapping me like swaddled child,
my cheeks warm and pink
as if that same sun kissed me now...
and believing I might shine someday
brightly and beautifully

but then that sun...

the sun is always above the clouds
you once said
and it is...
and always shining somewhere
He is determining when and where and how brightly
and how long the kisses may last...

you were close to me then
beside me even
as though you knew...
but then you always do.

Thoughts on the beach
October 2004

the wind is cold now
chills me through to my bones
the rustling leaves
sing their last songs before
they fall from the oaks
so lonely
softly
they dance with the wind
gracefully letting it lead

the shore is quiet
seagulls singing
sitting here by my blankets
waiting...
what will I share with them?

there's something melancholy about
today
even in all its beautiful peace
how my weariness has
caused me to sit quietly and soak
in all the sounds
scenes
fragrances
and made it difficult to
write them
and this quiet, crisp day

taking in the healing properties of the sea
my thoughts venture to Christ
and his
quiet
perfect way
when I wrestle with the
doubts that try to
overtake my peace

there in the distance
what's this I see...
my other self stands by the breakers
smiling
even shyly
and his eyes say everything
mysteries only my spirit understands
what a vision

the seasons are changing
here by the sea
my spirit feels quiet
peaceful
expectant
as though the season is changing
within me

welcome, change!
soft, lazy sunshine
kiss my heavy eyes
let me dream of my future

my season
leaves softly blowing
swirling
making the way for me
to move along

The Son Shines on This One
2004

there was a blossom
hidden, unable to spring forth
planted in rich soil
sweet rain falling
reviving...
and still...

small
struggling to see
beyond weeds...
only drinking a portion
of the sweet rain

You sent the sun
the clouds parted and the weeds
dried away
no longer stealing the sweetness
of the rain

that blossom
soaked up the sun and the rain
so hungry for more
blooming
vibrant colors
delicate fragrance
stronger stem
deeper roots...

and the sweet rain keeps
saturating
penetrating
liberating
while You look on
smiling
shining

take me with You
2003

take me deeper
take me to the place where
we become one
let me hear myself live
let me hear my heart
my breath
let me become aware of this very thing:
that I am alive

take me to the place
words cannot reach
where silence flatters and
makes a home for the essential
truth and peace
creating the heart of the matter

take me with You

Walk Forever by My Side
February 2005

the stones of the brook
are precious as gold
even the gold of Ophir
how many times I likened myself to one
felling giants...

speak to me
in silence
silence is golden
pure and sweet

stay forever by my side
only Your love
can release this pain I feel
break these chains
hold me close

smile on me and I will know
I am home

20 March 2005

I am not afraid
to fall into the arms of death
for in this
I will only come closer to You
there is none like You;
the Lifter of my head

I am not afraid
to face the terrible, unknown
to fight with all that is in me
until my weary bones
cry out for rest;
when I look to the hills
You are there

with a breath You can heal me
only You know the length of my days
the breadth of my life
You have numbered my days and
ordered my steps
You have promised me a long life
You have promised me the walled city

I am not afraid
of the very thing which tries
to take my life
break my spirit...
for You are greater

who is like You?

I am tired...
the pain overwhelms
in my exhaustion my mind wanders
and I am afraid
of living...
without purpose
without seeing the sands of
the Negev

I am afraid...
my enemy will defeat me
without You

h.e. newell

God

27 July 2004

sunshine
warming my face
like a thousand kisses
I've been missing
stepping out into the sun
as if for the first time
the waves
singing a song I
never knew....
everything is new
You've taken the old
made it new
sour is sweet again
because of You

Someday...

I feel like I could
be beautiful someday
if not today
all I need
is for You to look at me
to kiss me
to make me new

someday
I'll be beautiful
nothing else will matter
all Your promises will be with me
my son
my beautiful girls
Your man for me
destiny fulfilled
abundant life in you
gems in my crown
radiant

make me radiant with Your love
I so wish I was beautiful
dress me in crimson
anoint me with my favourite scent
pour spikenard over me
and wrap me in soft linen
oh won't You make me beautiful!

rest Your love
all over me
I want to shine

dance with me
I'm tired of dancing alone
my heart is breaking
it's broken

manifest Yourself to me
in the promise I hold fast to
soon
that I might know joy and love
that I might know
what it is to feel beautiful

Snow Falls on the Cedars of Lebanon
2004

catching
soft
cool
perfect...
dances on the wind
harmonies...

love falling
kissing my face
cheeks, chin, eyes...
rest in my hair like pearls
only for a moment
before you melt like wax

raise my hands to the One
who sends the promises
Promise Maker
Promise Keeper
tiny flakes touch my hands with care
like a lover...
here is love
dancing with me
around me
melting on me
refreshing this sleeping heart

what music is there?
what sound can describe the magic?
there is none
silence speaks loudly, clearly
smiles shine

this is the dance of
a thousand ages
the joy of the ageless One
deep within me
footprints circle in the white, soft...
manna? feathers?
who could feel the cold
when the dance is so deep...
manna falls on my tongue...
feathers fall on my face...
miracles surround me

like falling stars
I catch as many as I may
my spirit holding each one close
put them in my alabaster box
until I may pour them out for the one...
the only one...

here they are!
the tears which followed my prayers...
returned to me
no longer bitter...
but made sweetly perfect

2002

I see your face

in every crowd

hear your voice

in every room

precious

gentle

a lion and a lamb

leaning on your

heart

is my favorite place to be.

it always has

hope deferred

lies

manipulates

seduces

h.e. newell

nevermore

you never do

your sweet face

smiling

the silver moon

kissing

here am I

content

So Beautiful....
23 April 2010

Come near me
Beautiful One
terrify me...
I want to hold You
by the wounds in Your hands
breathe You in.

Hold me close
to Your open side
hide me in Your Love
breathe You in...
the Fire of your Holiness captivates me
breathe You in...
the sweet fragrance of Your Intercession
intoxicates me
breathe You in...
breathe You out...
over the Nations

Come closer, Cornerstone
terrify me...
I want to stand in the wounds
on Your feet
unmovable, You establish me
I stand firm in You

wind... wings...
living creatures watch
Spirit of God brings fire
tear-soaked altar blazes
wind... wings...

living creatures fan the flames
the Fire of Your Holiness
wind...wings...

I want to kiss
the wounds on Your head
burn your truth
on my lips
kiss them with my eyes open
see Your Crown, Humility
beauty undoing
terrifying

I can't look away
You're waiting for me to come closer to You...
I'm running...
terrified
undignified

Dark Sayings

Summer 2003

Oh, Lord!   You have sent forth your word.
There is no one like you.
Where can we go?
Where can we hide?
Who can seek shelter from the Lord?

There was a tree where the children hid from the sun.
They stayed in its shade and grew unhealthy
The hand of the Lord came down and pulled the tree
out of the ground.
The children fell in the hole and had nowhere to hide.
The sun shone on them, and their skin was so fair the
light shone through it.

I hear the Lord saying,
"The time is coming when all men will acknowledge
that they cannot hide from me.
That I see and know all.

That I shine upon them and make them well.
They will say in the shadows,
"The Lord will find us; we should just come out
for who can hide from the Lord?
The son of God has come
to shine light on all the earth.
Who can possibly avoid this?
The Light of the World was among us
and is coming back!"

And all will fall on their faces in terrible fear
for the splendor of the Lord will be undeniable.

August 2003
There was a candy maker who sold seven kinds of sweets.

People came and asked, "Why can you only make seven sweets?"

The man said, "I only have seven recipes. They are from my father
from long ago. I do not wish to learn more."

The people said, "Then we will go to the candy maker on the opposite side of the city. He makes more varieties, and his prices are better."

Days went by and the people began to become ill from the candy on the opposite side of the town. But out of pride, they continued to buy the less expensive candies.

After a time, the candy maker's brother said, "Come to my city and you will be able to sell you goods here."

So, the man went away and never looked back. The people are still ill and continue to eat the rotten sweets....

And this is what the Lord says.
"You have stayed to my course. My 'recipes' and directions have been good enough for you. Even when

those around you have compromised, you have stood your ground. You have stayed by me, and you have carried on the family name. Our vision has been kept alive in you:

quality

integrity

peace

grace

kindness

faithfulness

meekness

Because you have grown in these, I am increasing them in you. I am taking you to a new place and you will be respected there. I am sending out my Spirit to speak on your behalf to men, so they will see and know I am with you. In you. Working through you," says the Lord.

Summer 2004

A fruit farmer left his fields for one day. He set up a small stand in the city. He gave away many fruits to those who appeared to be hungry and without money to buy food. There were two men eating a grapefruit they had cut in half. The man on the left had a serrated spoon and he dug out the pulp and fruit neatly. The man on the right had a dull spoon and yet he made greatest efforts to get all the fruit and juice. So much so he was covered in juice and pulp...having fun eating it. The man on the left, however, discarded the fruit and ate the bitter rind. The man on the right took up his fruit and ate it with great delight.

The fruit vendor asked, "How did you like the fruit?"

The man the right was still eating, so he smiled and showed the farmer his hands full of fruit. But the man on the left said, "It was easy enough to peel; there wasn't very much to eat though."

The fruit vendor looked at the two men and considered them. Then he said to the man on the right, "I want you to come and work in my fields. I will give you all the fruit you wish to eat, and I will clothe you and feed you and give you provision. I'm only here for this day, so you have to decide now.

"The man on the right was so excited, he jumped up and left with the fruit vendor. As they walked away, the man left behind shouted after them, "Why does he get to go and not me? You see me sitting here with the same needs!"

The vendor said, "Because I gave you both the same sweet gift, the largest fruit I have. You chose to eat the rind, the outer shell. Good fruit you discarded, and never touched. This good man appreciates what was offered to him and received even your portion which you rejected. In the same way, I receive him and reject you."

The vendor took the man to his grove and cared for him all the days of his life. The man left sitting perished in his grief.

Open our eyes, Lord, to see what you are teaching us; to taste and see that you are good in all your ways.

Autumn 2003

There was a field and there were sheep in the pasture. At the far end were goats grazing on rocks because no one would let them near the grassy parts. The shepherd came and saw the goats. He wondered about them getting enough to eat to make milk for their babies, so he went to the father and asked, "Can you make a way for the goats to get fresh grass? Don't you have compassion on these goats just as you do the sheep?

The father said, "There is one who has an amount of grass to share with these goats. If the goats eat the grass, I will bless them and I will make them part of my flock."

So, the shepherd found this one and they gathered all she had set aside for the goats, and they went out and fed them.

And the Lord says, "The blessings of God are upon those who have mercy on even the unrighteous. I have poured out my spirit in this time, and I have poured it out on ALL flesh. ALL men. Blessed is the one who recognises this and moves accordingly. When you were goats yourselves, you were hungry, and someone fed you. Now is the time to offer fresh grass to the ones in the rocky places. NOW is the time to nurse the baby goats with sweet milk that they may grow and become lambs in my flock.

*"Those that withhold nothing from my goats, those that will humble themselves & give, serve them too, feed them also... those I will bless in abundance as they are so pleasing to Me.

**"Because if you don't go and feed them, who will go and feed them? Because I love them, too.

"There are none on this earth who fall so short of my grace they cannot still eat the baby food of my word.

When my people stop looking at reaching the lost as a telethon, then they will see fruit. When they stop looking at the lost with pity but with love, then they will see fruit."

(* and ** denotes a word added by another person)

3 March 2004
For the Watchmen

This is the word: there was a flock of birds like hawks, and they all had clipped wings. Local shepherds paid a man to keep their wings trimmed because they were afraid of the birds. One day the man who kept their wings clipped died suddenly. Their wings began to grow back, and they were able to fly over forests and pastures. They could see everything happening for miles.

The foxes in the woods became afraid as the birds' wings became stronger. Outside of the woods the foxes would be unable to hide now that the birds could fly, and they knew it. So, they went about getting twigs and grass, making something to hide under so they could get to the pastures undetected and steal the lambs.

When they came out of the woods, the birds were already able to fly. Their wings had grown very quickly, and they saw the foxes through the disguises. They swooped down and pulled it all off. The shepherds came and killed as many foxes as they could; the rest were driven back into the woods.

When the shepherds realized that the birds were able to fly and had saved the flock from being attacked, they began to weep and asked the birds to forgive them for clipping their wings.

The birds forgave them and flew away to the high places where they would be safe. They watched over the pastures from the high places for the rest of their days.

This is what the Lord says: There will come a time When their wings will grow faster than they can be clipped, and they will rise above and see the things the enemy is doing (watchman anointing).

They will step out and be called rebellious by man but know this: I have called them. I have sent them. I will always free them. I have made their wings and no man can clip them faster than I can make them grow. Shepherds will have no choice but to let the sharp-eyed birds grow. They will see they have been foolish, and they will repent.

These are my precious ones, and I am taking some of them to higher places. I am taking some of them away because I need them in other pastures. Be watchful for the season is coming when the oaks will be full of these birds whom I love so much.

(That's you guys. Watchmen being rejected and shut down. What an awesome God. He's redeeming you, us really. Man tries try to shut down prophetic (young) people, but God is raising you up, a Joshua generation

to take ALL the land the Lord has promised.
Land = every promise
God is awesome, in that you are another chance for a world that has sadly missed an invitation to be part of a great thing. Gideon's army has been called up for this season. But you, the precious (young) ones, the lovely birds... God sees and knows that you have a fresh, new desire for Him.
You are prophecy coming to pass. His gift to the lost and the religious, that they may be set free. Even though the shepherds repented, they were left, and the birds went higher.
birds = you lovely ones
Into the oaks
oaks = oaks of righteousness
  Like Isaiah 61. So, press in, because He is for you.)

Ezekiel 17:2

"Son of man, propose a riddle and tell a **parable** to the house of Israel."

Hosea 12:11 (TLV)

I also spoke through the prophets and I multiplied visions. Now through the prophets I will make **parable**s.

Psalms

27 November 2003

Oh, God, you are my protector and my shield.
Who is like you?
You are sovereign over all the earth, faithful and just to
all creation.
WHO IS LIKE YOU?
You search me, my God, and take away everything you
cannot use.
Everything I have opened doors to, or held on to
is yours to remove, I give it all to you.
Oh Jesus, save!

When I rise you are with me.
When I rise you have opened my eyes, and you have
breathed life into me yet another day.
WHO IS LIKE YOU?
When I stand and face the day, you are with me.
You are in front and behind me, beside me, within me,
nothing gets near me as long as I stand with you.
Let the oil of Gladness wash me cleanse me, make me

pure and holy again.
Let the oil of Gladness pour out upon my household.
The anointing breaks the yoke, the joy defeats the grief.
WHO IS LIKE YOU?
When I rise you have made a new day, fresh joy is welling up inside me.
Fresh hope, greater faith,
wake with me as I face the day.

Oh Lord, master, Adonai, you have marked me as yours, and I am grateful.
The awl in my ear was real, stung my flesh and pierced me.
WHO IS LIKE YOU!?
You removed my shackles and gave me bangles, anklets.
You removed my collar and gave me a necklace of silver.
You burned my rags and gave me white linen and purple robes.
You took my worn-out shoes and gave me sandals of leather.
Who is like you?

You have removed the curses and given me rest.
You have removed the history and given me my story;
my nights are spent dreaming now.
WHO IS LIKE YOU?
Fill my mind with thoughts of you and your sweet

salvation.
Fill my spirit with your presence.
Take my body and make it your temple.
PURE, strong, your resting place for all my days.
WHO IS LIKE YOU?
All I am is yours, for all I am is from you.
I would not have lived even in my mother's womb were it not for you.
Complete me the way you saw me before the beginning of time.
Mold me and shape me; I am yielding.
Your mighty hand upon me, make me a vessel, pure and open.
Only you can, Father.
Who is like you?

When you promise me that you will supply, I will wait.
When you promise me that I am victorious I will wait.
When you promise me that I shall go forth in your name, I shall wait.
When you promise, I shall believe you, and I shall wait.
Only you make unbreakable promises.
Only you can keep your word.
Only you shall I wait upon.
WHO IS LIKE YOU?
Only you know the desires of my heart.
Only you can give them to me.
Only you can promise them to me.
Who is like you?
Dreams come to me, Lord.

Revelations.
You warn me of the threat.
You share the coming blessings with me.
Who is like you?
Dreams stay with me throughout my day, fuel for prayer, food for faith.
How great a thing, to have you share such things with me.
Gentle and kind, you whisper to me while I sleep.
Who is like you?
Keep me rested, Lord, while I sleep.
You lay beside me and keep the enemy away.
There is a song in the night.
You put it in me, and I sing it for you!
WHO IS LIKE YOU?
Who gives such comfort?
Who gives such peace?
Who is like you?

Great as you are, you love me.
I am small and humbled by your affection.
Make me meek and mild, like my Jesus.
Make me a revolutionary like Him.
Who is like you?
Why did you choose me, oh God, with all my faults and short comings?
With all my fleshly ways, I have tried to help you and failed.
Yet you still call out to me.
You still trust me.

WHO IS LIKE YOU?
My heart is breaking, Lord, yet I have peace.
My soul is troubled, yet I have faith.
My mind is cluttered, yet I have clarity.
WHO IS LIKE YOU?
You spoke to me, you gave me a dream,
you gave me a hope, when I had none left.
Who is like you?

Prepare me to defeat this python.
What can stand against me when you are there?
You have covered my skin that I will not be bitten
You have strengthened my bones that I will not be crushed.
You have made me a giant that I may crush its head with my heal,
WHO IS LIKE YOU?
I saw myself pick it up and snap its spine, pull out its tongue.
In seven days, Lord, what will you do?
The python is weak.
I saw it come at my back, but you gave me speed and agility to move before her.
WHO IS LIKE YOU?
What will you do in seven days, Lord?
What will you cast down and what will you raise up?
I trust you, Lord, to do this in seven days.
You will remove the python.
Only you can.
WHO IS LIKE YOU?

Stay forever by my side.
Only you can cast a shadow over me.
Your shadow hides me, protects me.
Your kisses bind me.
Who is like you?
What man can set me free with a look?
What man can give me a song of salvation?
Who is man that he could give me living water?
THERE IS NONE LIKE YOU!

There is a man you have promised me.
He is a man seeking you.
Lord, you know him, you love him.
Surround him with your angels.
There is no one like you.
Call out to your man, Father, set him free.
Be his first love, his only joy.
There is no one like you.
Only you can show him this, Lord.
Only you can open his eyes to see.
Remove the scales.
Wipe away the venom the snake spit in his eyes.
There is no one like you.
Stay with me, Father, while my heart aches.
While I am still and trust that only you are God,
my banner, my provider and protector.
THERE IS NO ONE LIKE YOU!

Psalm for solidarity, unity and SHALOM within
18 October 2004

The Lord is good and worthy of our praises.
He is faithful beyond our imagination.
Praise the Lord every part of me;
praise Him even in the depths of my soul!
Praise Him every lock of my hair!
Every breath I take shall praise Him!
Every foot fall of mine will sing His Holy Name!

I cried out to the Lord:
Come down from your Holy Hill Oh God, and see me
here in my distress!
Come down from your lofty place
and rescue me from my lament!
My heart is heavy with darts and tar
that I have been unable to remove myself.
Oh you, Jehovah Rophe!
Do not consider the pain of my affliction
but only the joy of my freedom
as you heal me!

In my desperation I was spurned by men.
I was scorned like David by Michal
when I bared all before my God and my peers
many rebuked me and called me faithless.
How can men know where my faithfulness lies?
How can they scold me for my frustration?

Surely I am not alone in my despair

From the heavens came a sound;
a voice like thunder and trumpets
and a thousand buzzing bees.
My ears filled with warm oil.
My face dripped with oil and my head
touched the floor in fear and shame,
but the voice of the Lord spoke at last to me
like a gentle lover against my ear.

"Where are you daughter of Zion?
and why are you clothed in rags and filthy?
Why are you perfumed with shame and despair
and filled in your belly
with sour milk and stale crumbs?"

Oh my God!
Lord of heaven and earth,
break every union I have had with my enemy;
forgive me for coming to agreement
with his lies.
Forgive me, oh King, for letting him clothe me
when my Lover has given me such fine garments!
I have been adulterous.
I have fluttered my eyelashes at my enemy
and received his trinkets.

"Where is your Lover, daughter of Zion?

Where is He now?"

My Lover is here.

"Yes.
Always here."

Yes

"Look here, you daughter of Zion;
look to the east to city of your father, David,
and here will be your comfort.
Lift up your head, you child of covenant.
I am faithful to my word
and you will see the scoffers
stand behind you in repentance
when you enter the city gates
clothed in all your beauty,
in the splendor of my beauty.
Stand daughter, preparing for her moment
and know that I am with you;
even elevating you because you are faithful

"Why do you call me from my Holy mountain
when I have given you favor
to approach me without invitation?
Spit out the stone in your mouth,
the fear of loving me.
Let the sweetness of your voice
calling my name be heard in my ears.

There is no restriction upon you.
I love you in my presence;
I long for you there.
My gates are open to you always;
I wait to hear you coming,
to kiss you as you enter my lofty place."

Glory to the Holy one of Israel!
He has delivered me from my shame
and brought me back to my place.
He has removed the blinders from my eyes
and caused my enemy to flee.

Glory to the Lord, Adonai Nisi!
He has covered me with His love,
His banner and standard protect me.
He is the God of my salvation.
He has brought me into covenant with Himself
and all other covenant is void.

Glory to the Lord, the Promise Maker,
for He has been faithful
and I have found favor in His sight.
His Son has kissed me with the kisses of His mouth
and I am set free.

Glory to the Lord, the God of Righteousness!
He will meet me in the Holy place;
He will meet with me on the slopes of Mt Hermon

where the oil of gladness will cover my face
forever.

My Psalm.
December 2003

oh Lord, you are my saving grace.
your mercy saved me from the dark,
your peace calmed my troubled heart,
your justice goes before me,
and your vindication covers me.
with your right hand
you lifted me out of my despair;
all I can do is praise You

let me weep at Your feet.
let my tears wash Your feet.
here I bring my alabaster box
to the foot of Your throne;
I pour myself out here.

all I have to give is my shame and my pride,
like doves to lay upon Your altar.
a sacrifice to remember Your
great faithfulness,
Your loving kindness.
send me anywhere, ask of me anything
and I can only submit.

You take the bitter salt of my tears
and turn them to sweet wine.
you take the sour foulness
of my sin and shame

and give me spikenard in return.

how shall I worship the God of Mercy?
what can I offer the King of Kings?
who else but the Lord who makes you Holy
shall I cry out to?

let your praises be forever on my tongue!
let your praises constantly fill my heart!
make my life a sacrifice of praise;
a pure and worthy sacrifice of praise.
never leave my side!
never remove your name from my lips!

all the days of my life
let me worship You.
all that I hold precious
let me give to You.
even as I stand alone
let me glorify You in all I do!

h.e. newell

A Song for Shiloh
August 2004

Let us walk the road to Shiloh!
Let us step lively as we travail;
the Lord is at Shiloh waiting for us!
the Lord Most High, the Holy One is waiting
waiting in His lofty place smiling down on the vineyards
of His beloved Shiloh.

Now I anoint myself with the fine fragrances
of the flowers of these fields;
with myrrh and cinnamon and rosewater.
Join me and make a fragrance for the Lord!

Now I make myself adorned with soft pearls
and silver bangles and agate stones,
and a ring in my nose where my Lord claimed me
for unity with His son!

Now I wear my white linen robes,
fine and soft and layered seven times...
and my veil of fine gauze so that I may not
look upon another while my lover waits for me!

Now I take off my sandals,
so that my lover may wash my feet
when he has found me and taken me home.
Nothing from my journey may stay once He has found

me.

Now I wear the silver bells that sound my coming
so my lover will know where to find me.
My body will make a joyful noise as I dance
in the vineyards at Shiloh, and worship my King.
The virgins will follow the sound of it and find the winepress;
my lover will be there waiting!

My spirit is already there,
in the Holy place, the Lofty Place of the Lord!
His banner covers me
and I am safe, hidden, content to be with Him here,
in the place of His habitation;
the place of restoration.

Let us go to the valley with glad hearts!
For the presence of the Lord is there;
His dwelling place and His Holy tabernacle!
The heavens have opened up and revealed the glory of the Lord,
and the glory of the Lord smiles upon Shiloh for us!

Hadassah's song
2004

Oh bless the Lord my soul!
bless Him in His sanctuary!
I will bless the Lord with everything I am
for He has done great things
my heart has filled to overflowing
with the great love of my King
and as I stand preparing I cry out
with songs of joy and peace.

How much longer will I prepare
to stand in your presence?
How much longer will I prepare
to bring my petition before you?

My heart yearns to stand in your presence
to kneel before your throne
to pour out to you.
From my chambers where I wait in the quiet
I cry out to you
From behind my veils I flutter my eyelashes at you.
All I see is you
and you are all I desire!

Oh sisters... bathe me in spices
anoint my hair with fine oils,
and trim my robes with pearls
Let me stand in the presence of my king

in the splendor of His majesty
Let me please him as I come before him
let his heart break for me

Oh Lord, you alone are my fragrance
you alone are my veil
you and only you are my string of pearls
bring me into your chambers oh my Love
for I am only for you
Keep me sealed up in your heart
and wear me like a seal on your arm,
like a badge on your breast
Let me find favor in your eyes oh my King,
and never leave that place.

Oh sisters, how will you stand before the king?
rejoice and be glad when your hour comes!

Dying to self so you are glorified
2004

Oh Lord how long will you wait!?
How long will you allow me to slip
and sink in this mud?
How long will I stay in the cistern?
Where is your mighty right hand?
Where is the God of my fathers?

Oh Adonai, you are sovereign
how long will you allow me to rule
my own life
to be in agreement with these lies?
How long oh my Lover,
will you allow me to be a rebellious
adulterous fool?
When will you break my will
conform it to yours so that
I may end this cycle of despair.

My hope is in you, Mighty One!
My life is in the God of the angel armies!
My faith is in the Lord the God who saves!
My desire is to be pure and right
before Him all the days of my life
to be His and His alone
submitting to no other spirit or man
only His Spirit in me,
only His man for me.

He Prepares a Table for Me 75

Rise up Daughter of Zion
rise up and face your enemy.
Rise up Daughter of Zion
face the darkness and see the light.
How long will you fight Me?
How long will you hold on to the old
when I stand waiting with the new?

Greater and lovelier times are ahead
The city of gold is waiting
for the Daughter of Zion,
the prince awaits his princess
the land awaits you
take your portion in the land
you Daughter of the King of the universe!
The golden road from Tirzah to Susa
will know your scent as you walk it
as you enter the city of Esther.

How will you say that I am a God who
makes no promises to you?
How will you say that your lot is meager
and your life is without purpose?
How will you say that I have given you to the nations
yet given you nothing in return?
My heart grieves to know that
you have found me unfaithful,
to know that you have chosen to eat stones
when I have already shown you
the sweetness of figs.

Oh Daughter of Zion
how long will you walk blindly?

The Lord is good
my heart knows the goodness of the Lord
He has sent His Salvation from
His holy habitation
and pulled me from the snares set for me.
He has taken me in and clothed me
He has bathed and fed me
when I was hungry and filthy in my iniquity.
My mind fights to remain
snared and snagged
clothed in rags and sackcloth
while my spirit rejoices before the Lord!

Be glorified Oh my God
be victorious in my life, sovereign
not my will but yours!
Break me so that only you remain
be glorified in all I do
let my life be a testimony of your healing power
your compassion and grace.

Wipe out my words my King
the decrees I have made against you
the curses I have placed upon myself
make my confession a beautiful song
and my very walk a dance of worship.
Let those who see me say:

look at the good work the Lord has done!
Look how the Lord has taken her out of the pit,
like Joseph,
and fulfilled the dreams He gave him,
because she has learned a lesson of value!

Oh Jehovah, be my peace,
let me know you are still with me
Please do not take your seal from my forehead
only love me, have mercy on me,
for I am still a foolish child
and I am your child, a child of covenant.

h.e. newell

Jan 2005

worship the Lord in the beauty of His holiness
look to the heavens with expectation

build an altar
He will come

on the slopes of Mt Hermon
I will lift up my hands
to the King of Glory
my face will shine like the sun
my robes will be oily
and my feet wet
under my feet the mountain will say
"Glory to the Lord on High!"

come with me to the high place
let us see the Lord of hosts
He is calling and I shall answer
come up and see
with me

Psalm for the staff of the Lord
16 June 2005

Let me lift up Your name in the highest place.
Let me rejoice at the sound of Your breath on my ear.
Let me sing with all that I am,
"Make a joyful noise all the earth
make a noise all your own all you creatures on the earth;
stars shine,
waters ebb and flow,
wheat fields yield in the wind
as your noise exalts the Most High!"

How can I say that You haven't raised me up?
How can I say that You sleep when I am mourning?
Let me tell the whole of Creation about the
wonderous love of the Lord,
the King of all Creation!
Sing, oh mouth, let the song in my heart
be heard in the highest places in the clouds;
in the lowest places under the seas.
Dance, oh feet, let all my footsteps lead me
closer and closer to the Throne of the Jasper God!
Let them dance upon injustice
and create a pathway for the lost.

Set my hands upon your altar, oh Holy One,
consume them in the fire of Your Holiness
so that I may be worthy to carry the rod which You

have handed me.

Let that rod bloom!
Let it be so heavy with almonds that I
rely on You to carry it with me,
through me.
How can I walk without the staff of the Lord?
How do my legs hold me up in the presence of the Lord?
Your mercy is greater than my life
it is You who holds me up and guides my feet!
Let me sing always of the gentle mercies of You;
let me sing let me sing, let me sing!

From a Journal

31 October 2004

Cape May, NJ

Once at a Todd Bentley conference, while sitting up in the balcony with the girls and a friend of mine, I actually *felt* the whirl wind of God. From the podium, Todd looked up and said, "You! Put your hair over your face, God is coming to you NOW!" Being the insatiable child I am, I flipped that hair over my face and threw my hands up in the air... I wanted it all!

As Todd spoke the word of the Lord into my spirit, I was caught up in the whirlwind, shaken, rearranged, and transformed. "... and you will come up and see!... open heavens... Throne room..." Thank goodness I recorded the meeting. My daughter held down my skirt, the guy below us apparently thought I would go over the balcony, and my girl fell beside me on the floor. I have never been the same since. I love the way God does His thing!

There's something about time away... it re focuses you on your vision, and helps you get what is being birthed through the membrane of that stubborn nature we call "self". These last days have been like this for me. I remembered the way I used to ask my ex-husband could we please get stationed in Utah or someplace so I could go to the desert like Moses and Jesus... I wanted transformation! of course the Navy has no need of a shipyard in Utah...
Thinking about Scott's e mail, and the Fresh Fire conference, I recalled Sil, the boy I prayed with on the street later that night. He was from a tough place... and he was so hungry for God! We started to pray with him, and some friends of his... and I knew there was something... I wasn't clear to go yet...

I put one hand on his head, one on his back and started getting aggressive... This boy wanted a breakthrough, and I wanted to see him get it! After all, God wanted to also, and Christ paid for it... As he began to repeat after me, "I am a new creation, He sees Himself in me!", the weeping came and then the shift in the spirit. As he spoke it louder and louder and with more authority. you could FEEL it, the breakthrough. Here this child, who had seen the toughest aspects of gang life by the time he was 15, was curled up in a ball on the sidewalk, releasing the pain, receiving healing, being transformed.

This is what the power of God can do for a life. This is how, in seconds, the love of Christ can reverse a life of abuse and violence and redeem that life. This is where the pursuit of holiness bears good fruit; when lives are changed... To this day, Sil has done nothing but continue to grow in Christ, and it has been a beautiful thing to be part of. This is my desire: to live this life of purpose...

"Come up and see," the Lord had said. "*Jacob's ladder*!" He'd promised. awesome, isn't it?

Sometimes I get so far, and I get comfortable there. I forget that there's a long way to go before I reach the top of this ladder. He brings me deeper into Himself, and reminds me that in comparison, I know nothing. Where I came from is miles away, and yet where He's taking me is always now. I love this about Him.

During my time away, I went to see my friend in Delaware. It was quiet time, and we enjoyed peaceful conversation and a great dinner. Sharing some of what I do with him was strange at first, but as I sat with him and forced myself to be open, God spoke to me: "This is what I made you, this is who you are". From there, it became easy to be open and not care how kooky it sounded. We talked about the things I have been dealing with, and how they've been very raw, like open cuts, and how I didn't understand this... He shared his gentle wisdom with me, reassuring me that I am not so strange for going through it. We spoke about some of the experiences I've had in ministry, and other things, and about strange dreams and occurrences he's had as well. During it all, clarity of vision, which we also spoke about, returned to me.

I want a Moses experience, and I want to be free, in this lifetime. For me, ME, to live a life of purpose, to live the love of Christ, there must be a sacrifice, and there must be a purging. My mantra is the Word, my focus; to be His vessel, my purpose; to glorify Him. Nothing and no one can come before it.

I miss the lil waxes, but this quiet time has been a powerful time of reflection... I've spent almost the whole time in prayer, contending for this breakthrough, so I can continue to climb the ladder. And just like with Sil, the tangible release of it all came.

I had to go through it, like some kind of pity party for one, so that I could see how far I've come, and how far I have yet to go. You have to let more baggage go, so you can get deeper into that awesome place He has for us, the intimacy, the freedom, the presence...

Moses had to take his sandals off simply to approach a bush! and as he knelt in the presence of God there, he was transformed, leaving everything behind from his travels (dirt on his shoes...). In the end, Moses gave up everything, to fulfill His purpose, only to have it restored in abundance. My Yeshua entered this world leaving everything behind... to come in the frailty of a man and leaving everything behind on earth. He went into His ministry, even unto dying for me, leaving everything again. Is it too much to ask, that I; small, little me, leave all my travel baggage behind to go deeper into the secret place? Hardly. comparatively, my sacrifice is skimpy, but it's mine, and He requires it.

This is the essence of love, unconditional, and pure. This is the essence of compassion, deep and compelling. It expects nothing; requires everything; and manifests freedom. This is love that knows not emotion, but depth. This is Him, in me, teaching and shaping me. And this same love, which motivated my Lord to fulfill prophecy so I may live, must motivate me.

I learned over these past few days, that words are secondary. My 'job' obviously requires me to speak quite a bit at times. These words must always speak of His love in me and express His love for others. He cherishes me, and He hides me in His heart, and I must love others this same way. Whether it's my children, my mom, strangers at churches I minister at, or friends, this love is the focus. Anything else is my own invention, and not His. Intellect and ego have no place in this walk I am on. My mind, even in its healthiest state, can be my worst enemy, especially as it divides... As it seems to have been lately... My thinking, my philosophy, will, understanding, desires, emotions... ALL must conform to His will. there will be no rest for these bones until the breath of Life blows on them again. This will be a repeated process as long as I live.

The ladder isn't just for me. The bones don't climb it without muscles and tendons to cause action...and there will be a continued process of burning and re-storing, until He sees me as finished. It's a good thing this fasting time. I feel healthier (in many ways) than I have in a long time, and focused, which is great. and more will come as I press in and hold Him to act on my behalf, for His namesake :)

Everything is left to Holy Spirit at this point. I have to see this through.

20 September 2006

An epiphany came to me this morning while I was mopping the floor and listening to Kirk Bennett. Mahala and I were talking about dreams earlier, and what it means when you dream that your teeth are falling out. I have always understood it as an indication that God is about to, wanting to, or in the process of rearranging my wisdom and understanding, so I shared the same with Mahala. Not thirty minutes later, I had a fresh revelation of the amazing and unique creative power of our God.

So often, I ponder the way John in Revelation 4 sees God. Colors, rainbows, light. And as I heard those words in the prayer again, I realized freshly, that all that creative power and beauty is wrapped up inside of us. The Uncreated One graciously deposits the indescribable beauty that John saw in us all. He gave the same jasper wonder to Adolf Hitler, Golda Meir, Ted Bundy, Oral Roberts, you, and me, Judas, Moses... You will never find anyone in the history of creation that God chose to leave that aspect of His likeness out of. Now my awe is twofold; the amazing generosity of the Lord to share His creative beauty with us, and the unconditional way He has created all people in the faith that they would choose Him over all things.

Creation miracles are so much more than sperm meeting egg and a nine-month metamorphosis. There is the unequalled intimacy of the breath of God meeting with a tiny sliver of His Rainbow and the two becoming one as they reach down into the womb to join the physical. For an instant, I saw and understood this amazing marriage of Creator, spirit and flesh. For an instant, I again realized the utter speechlessness John had when He saw the Jasper God.

No wonder God creates us in the dark secret of the womb! Who could see all that perfect light, all that beautiful color and not be blown away? How else could He have perfect communion with us in our physical condition except to hide us away in the secret place of our mothers for 9 months as He speaks all things into us? I think even mothers on drugs, or who have consecrated their infants to Satan cannot even keep God away from this beautiful communion time.

Who could?

Deep calls to deep. The womb is deep, the deepest place in our creation journey. Destinies revealed there, gifts, names, talents, beauties given. The Word is made flesh there, and we have perfect understanding of it for the only time in our lives, because we are not yet corrupt. All the light and color of the Lord is swirling around that tiny precious life within the womb of a woman, and He is delighting in it. I am convinced that beyond the scientific or medical explanations of fetal movement, is the glorious dance of Spirit and spirit that science cannot know.

My emotions have progressed during this pregnancy from numbness and near depression, to a serene and supernatural kind of joy. Even in my numb condition I was determined not to feed the spirit of this little one any kind of venom and I pray that I have not. Somehow, in this fifth month, revelation and love are flowing back into me, and I am ecstatic. My teeth seem to be falling out and everything I thought I understood about the Beauty and Vastness of our God seems so obsolete.

Here is the marvelous mystery of the miracle of Creation: that the Lord in His unending complexity shares with the world, through each of us, a piece of His Beauty and Power. Just as all of my children are unique and have some aspect of my nature in them, they each enrich this mortal life on earth in their own ways, as we all do in the plan of the Almighty Father. Within me now grows the Beauty of the Lord in human form. How blessed I feel to understand that now.

Thunder, drums, trumpets, voices. I watch, as the rhythm of Heaven becomes a heartbeat, a pulse in the veins of the created one, spoken into him by the King of Heaven. The rhythm of Heaven. The song of God. Who else can know the song of Heaven but the creatures on the earth who walk in obedience at all times?

The miracle within the secret place of the womb knows it; it's the only song that life knows. This is the heartbeat that doctors see as a sign of life at fourteen weeks gestation, but we can be sure that this heartbeat has been beating since before the time before time.

28 August 2006

(Grace never dies)

Websters gives several definitions of grace in its listing, one of which being: delay granted for payment of an obligation. I like to call that mercy. Being covenant breakers, we have been given the most outstanding gift of mercy imaginable, in that Jesus Christ took on our sin and paid the price for all our sin and rebellion. He became sin for us and made it possible for us to return to the covenant relationship with God and know His unique and perfect Grace. Sometimes I cannot get my mind around this undoing truth, and I am broken down to a place where it becomes fresh and fundamental revelation to me again.

The Grace (love and favor) of God is all around us. It is evident moment by moment, breath by breath, in everything we see and everyone we meet daily. How can we look at the delicately balanced earth we live on, and not recognise His marvelous love and kindness? Our Creator provides us all we need to survive: air, water, shelter, food, and all we need to live: the privilege of eternal intimacy with Him. Yes, surviving and living are in fact two different things, and we can know the two only if we have accepted the invitation God gives us through His Son, Christ Jesus.

When I think about the simple and perfect plan that we

are part of in this huge universe, I am overwhelmed with emotion. Having done nothing but ask forgiveness and commit to a life of obedience, we are given access to the very same riches the Creator of all things has in His own hands. Every creature has a purpose. Prior to the fall, everything was simply here for the enjoyment of the Lord, the Word, and the Spirit. Now everything fights for survival, even the plants and elements must fight for their right to live. All of these things live in obedience to the Lord. Mountains stand and divide, oceans roar and balance land temperatures, the moon orbits and draws tides... animals keep the continuous circle of life rotating in their own communities. It seems that man, the only creature given a mind to reason and a spirit to commune with the Throne Room of Heaven, is the only creature who repeatedly breaks the heart of God Himself.

This is where I see grace the most; in that we are still here in spite of our rebellion and disobedience.

Violent Grace brought us back into covenant with the King of the Universe. The Darling of Heaven gave Himself over to sacrifice for us, because He would rather have died a horrible agonizing death for every person who would live and die from that moment on, than live a second in Paradise without any of us. Forgiveness was poured out - and continues to pour Itself out - even over the foulest of people. The blood of the Lamb never dries up, it never congeals or stops flowing. How can the Eternal One ever stop? Grace never sleeps, It can't rest until every chance a person has is exhausted and they are either in Heaven or Hell. Grace is a river of pure and beautiful blood that washes over everything in Its path. No one can escape or elude the power of Grace, only reject it. And perhaps what I find the most amazing aspect in the nature of God's Grace is this very truth: Grace is so persistent It never stops offering Itself to us no matter how many times we reject It.

I believe that one way we can know who is truly teaching the pure and complete gospel of Grace is to observe how gentle and humble the Grace they are sharing is. Jesus never walked among the pagans and thought them too filthy to care for. Holy Spirit does not terrorize people into repentance. God does not conditionally love His children; of this I am most confident. My belief is that like all parents, He has a natural and deep love for us all regardless of our spiritual condition, and that He requires us at some point to become accountable and committed to Holiness and Salvation.

There is no favoritism in the family of God, simply various levels of intimacy and obedience; true Grace recognises this. Jesus never manipulated or judged everyone in those last breaths on the Cross, He loved, interceded, and longed for all. Grace was not choosey or proud in those hours or at any other time, It spoke for everyone and so should we. This is the Gospel we should live and die for, teach and preach, share and spread no matter what it costs us.

Let me just say this about the never-ending flow of Blood that eternally flows from the Cross. Only God can stop the flow of it. Only He can determine the day and time that the River will cease to flow and His Judgement will come instead. None of us can ever presume to know when that hour will be, and this is another way we can know those who are truly focused on Christ and His Grace first and foremost from those who are serving another master. For these also the flow of Grace from the Cross never ends, Jesus is still waiting for them as He did for us who still often struggle with our loyalties.

Jan 27, 2005

Zechariah 9:12 (TLV)

*Return to the stronghold, you prisoners of hope!
Today I declare that I will restore twice as much to you.*

sometimes things look far away... bleak, frustrating... you know you're reaching for something, and it seems so close, yet so far away...

why is it far away? are we pushing it away, and without any good reason? is it pushing us away? is it here and we're so used to asking for it that we can't see it?

Mae's head is totally better... it was better by yesterday morning, no bump no red, no pain. that's awesome. signs and encouragements come all the time... I spoke to a friend of mine I haven't spoken to in a while... and I asked Him to make some restorations there... we have half our paperwork sorted to leave... it's little things that make your faith stay alive.

last night I slept lying down the first time in months. no pain, no nothing, just sleep. now THAT is a sign that He's working. I dreamed beautiful dreams, and I saw... my other self. perhaps he is close?

we cannot look at the outward way of things. we must

seek to find the small glimpses of hope... the small fruits of our prayers. if I looked upon every situation with my natural eyes, I'd have killed myself a long time ago. we all would have. it's hope and faith that keeps us strong.

we can only be concerned with doing and saying what He has set out for us to do and say. everything else is secondary, and most of it isn't our responsibility. I'm not told to make anyone do anything, and their reaction to my words and deeds is their business. I have enough to be concerned about. and anyway, God is still in control of everything...

the Word says, "today" He's restoring... that doesn't mean it's not happening, just because the finished work is unseen. that means that even as I type this, He is moving, and working in wonderful ways... I cannot see. things can't always look wonderful, or I would have no need for faith, or God...

sometimes the waiting is the hard part, and sometimes it's sweet. bittersweet... you must have joy in the journey, you have to have sorrow... they each make the other have purpose.

I keep songs in my head, and praise on my tongue... He gives me peace, and scriptures... and I stay in my prayer closet... my tallit is getting good and soaked... this is a season where the things He has promised are closer than we know, I believe. and even if they aren't... living in faith and hope beats the alternative...

at least in this corner it does...

14 April 2005

When I think of the awesome, undoing power of God, I am speechless. How can we find words to describe the very thing that renders us selfless and causes us to become holy like Him? Try as we might, we cannot find a word to match or describe it, for His mind is so infinite and ours so small, in comparison grains of sand.

What is more intriguing to me is His generosity. He is so extravagant in how He shares His holiness with His friends, for we need a measure of it to understand Him and be able to survive His presence. Royalty relates to royalty, and we as grafted in heirs to the Kingly inheritance must learn how to relate to the King. No earthly king has an endless supply of anything, so we are fortunate beyond our understanding that our King is so wealthy and willing to share it.

Because of the love with which He gives His gifts, we can know there is no manipulation behind Him. And this is the very thing we understand the least: why does He give us everything when we give Him so little? Do I even desire to love the Lord with all of me? Holiness, if it is growing inside me and taking strong roots, should cause me to want to love God with everything I have and everything He has. Could there be some unreached part of me that recoils at the thought of holiness? Let it die if it lives, for I have only one magnificent obsession: to love holiness even if I must die because of it.

When Jesus came, and was holiness on earth, how could people have hated Him so much? Perhaps it is because they hated holiness so much, they could not even see that they hated it. Is this why He called them of their father Satan? I think so, and because of this I strive even harder to know my Sonship and love it.

I have been reading about church reformers and how they were called evil and heretical because they wanted holiness to thrive among their people. John Knox declared to the heavens "give me Scotland or I will die", and He stood up even to a Queen who hated righteousness. Holiness brings integrity, excellence of character. Jesus had the most excellent character of us all and died because of it. We should be willing to do the same because He loved us first.

Sometimes I wonder why the Lord doesn't simply impose His holiness on some. Of course, such a thing would contradict His very nature, and so He offers it freely and the willing receive it. Can we be surprised by the way His holiness in us incites hate in those who have rejected it in the first place? Hardly, and for this reason our souls must cry out as Christ's did, "forgive them Father..." while they crucify us. How can I reach this level of love for my brothers? Surely holiness is the only way.

If we can find no words to express the awesome power of His love and holiness, is it possible that there are none? Are we able to articulate the grief the Spirit of God feels when It sees us rejecting and persecuting one another? No. I'm certain we cannot, for if we could, we would die from the pain of it. Perhaps in our human condition we would also die if we had a complete understanding of His holiness. Isn't this why Moses turned his head and watched the Lord's back? This is the great mystery of it.

I am left to ponder the holiness of God in new ways as He reminds me that it is a gift of love; a wedding gift to create a pure and spotless bride. In His holiness I am free indeed to love my Bridegroom and detest any other perverse lover who may try to distract me. He has told us to love what is good and holy, and I will love it more than my life. when I get to paradise, He will tell me what words describe His holiness. Of course, by then it won't matter.

From a Writing Class

Summer 2016

Somehow a likeness of my fifteen-year-old daughter made it to the soft, blue sofa, giving me a full display of what the "Spice" did to her. Realizing now, what had gone on behind my back for months, I kept telling myself not to go near her, in case I really did lose my temper. I buried my nose in the paper I was feverishly trying to rewrite, hoping it would help.

Nothing did.

My mind was a perfect storm of emotions and blame. I was completely alone, dealing with yet another crisis.

All this time, my usually sweet girl rocked, cackled and babbled as one possessed. She sounded like a demon. I could hardly think for having to babysit my hallucinating child. She got up once or twice following things that weren't there and believing she needed to go check on her little sister. I'm not sure what ticked me off more, the fact that I knew she'd lied to me and used the stuff again, or the fact that it was part of our lives in the first place.

With all the subtlety of a shotgun blast, Charlie texted. "My girlfriend's out of town so I'm drinking her wine and texting you."

I came painfully close to telling him that he was reminding me why I'm still single. Instead, I just blocked him; he didn't deserve to know what I was dealing with. I didn't want his prayers.

Almost immediately Cindi stopped by, just curious to see what was on for tea.

I sobbed on the front stoop, vomiting all my anger and frustration at her feet. Like the true friend she is, she listened without complaint.

"God knew," she smiled. And He really did. She walked past me and sat on the soft, blue sofa with the thing who resembled my child. She sat, smiling, praying for my sweet girl. All the patience I didn't have had been allotted to Cindi in spades, and I suddenly felt guilty for being so angry. For feeling alone. He is always a step ahead.

Around midnight I finished the paper and looked up from the laptop to find my child sleeping where the half ghoul sat earlier. Cindi, still smiling, untangled herself from my unconscious daughter and covered her with a blanket. It was my Klimt blanket, and I struggled between tearing it off her and tucking her in so tightly she'd be restrained. Doing neither, I kissed her face instead.

After Cindi left, I sat at the table and shook my head, unable to name anything I was feeling. Watching that stuff possess my child, I knew that in spite of the long, infuriating night, she needed me to hate the drugs not her. She needed me to trust Jesus on her behalf.

"I love her more than I hate that stuff," I sighed, choosing. My thumb hovered over the contact number of the chief of police. My eyes burned with exhaustion. The strategy planning could start in the morning.

Somehow, I made it to the soft, blue sofa and cuddled my beautiful daughter for the rest of the night.

The Night the Light Wouldn't Change

2003

Cape May is an interesting place. The whole town is a historic landmark, which bursts at the seams with people in summer. As kids we'd go to the promenade in front of convention hall, decked out in some kickin' clothes, and hang out until all hours. Some things haven't changed.

In summer of 2003, I had a fractured ankle. Talk about no fun. For about a week it became terribly hot, and having no air conditioner, I took Jael and Mahala to a movie one night. Michael Caine is cool, and even cooler in Second Hand Lions. Having enjoyed the great movie and the cool air, we decided to walk out on the promenade. And there I saw her; Amber I think was her name.

There are moments in your life when you just see yourself. You see yourself in the past and you are in awe. Amber was one of those moments. Such a pretty girl, sandy hair, pretty face, nice figure, black fishnet tights, black t-shirt and a little black skirt... The Lord said to me, "You need to go talk to her." Now, of course I came up with every excuse why I couldn't at the moment. I was sweaty, the kids were tired, my foot hurt... So, I hobbled down the ramp to the street and decided to go home.

We had waited at the light for some time when one of the girls said, "Mom, shouldn't the light have turned?"

Have you ever felt like Jonah? I looked to my right, and there was the girl the Lord had showed me to speak to. Ok, so now I knew the light was not going to change for me anytime soon. I had a vision of every light along Beach Ave staying red until I spoke to this girl... I hobbled over to the embankment... Jael and Mahala just sort of leaned on it, waiting. One of her friends called her over and she climbed down. Looking her in the face was like looking in my own eyes, and sure enough, poor kid, the first thing out of her mouth was: "Am I in trouble?"

"No, honey, you're not. I'm a Christian and when I look at people God shows me things. And He told me to come over here and tell you that you are really a beautiful girl, and He loves you. He wouldn't even let me cross the street until I came to speak to you."

What a thing it is to see the whole face, the spirit of a person change.

"He loves the way you have so much joy, and He hears you when you talk to Him."

"He does?" was the puzzled response.

"Yes, He sure does, sweetie." and I hugged her. And to

the stunned face, the shock and surprise that had the tiniest hint of 'why me?' to it, I said, "You know something? When I was your age, I looked just like you do, except my hair was blue." There it came, the rest of the wall. She smiled the prettiest smile. And then the light changed. "You be blessed, precious, you and your friends."

On the way home the girls and I talked about that girl, and the way she reminded me of me. I was always called fat, or freak, and I truly thought I was ugly and fat, even at 140 pounds. All through my teens, the years where I should have been growing into who I am, the liar had me thinking I was nothing. I was being beat down by the enemy. Just like Amber was. No prophetic person spoke truth into my life like that back then. Prophetic words don't have to fill books. That tiny word of encouragement may have really broken some things off her at that moment.

That's why He kept the light red. It was a statement to the enemy: Thus far and no farther!

Everyone Needs a Hug

29 January 2004, Wildwood

Today panned out to be better than I thought it would. Seems like when days start out a little crazy, this is the case. Of course, I just got home from church, the seminar began tonight... it was soooooo good. Especially the praise time. the drums... I just knew they were calling me. You know how I love drums during worship... And then this woman walked in... I hadn't seen her before.

Tall, thin, pretty lady, sat down in the back. She sat with a man and began to wail and weep. Poor thing, so sad. I mean she was BROKEN and didn't care who knew it. She laid down on the floor at one point crying out...then she walked around...and after a while I could see she was drunk or something. Her eyes said it all.

And then He said, "She needs a hug."

I have become, for many reasons lately, unaffectionate. But He has had me hug people before, sharing His love with them, so this was no new thing. As I went to her, she was starting to leave, and I said, "God just told me to hug you, may I?" I can tell you, in my whole life, I have never held anyone so desperate, so absolutely broken...

She sank into my arms like an anvil on a hammock. We stood, in the corner in the back, and I just held her... What else could I do? She wreaked of alcohol and smoke...and she clung to me like it meant her very life, sobbing and wailing. And I just sang over her, holding her, praying...sharing with her all I saw and heard. With each word I spoke, she sank deeper into me, sometimes sobbing, sometimes almost screaming. It was obvious, all she needed to know was that He was still with her...

"He saw you when your man walked out..." And she sobbed even harder.

"He doesn't care whether your drunk or what, He sees it's a struggle." Followed by a deeper squeeze of my back... At times like these, you just don't care what a person smells like, or what anyone thinks of it all. People hurt, and they need to know it's ok to hurt.

This man, it turns out was her father, stood at the back of the church, weeping. "Oh, please help my baby!" he was saying. All the love in his eyes, the sorrow of seeing his child, a grown woman, so broken... Just there, nothing to hide. Everyone was praising, and I just kept quietly singing, holding her up, loving her the way He asked of me. Hugging her in His place, squeezing out all the junk, the hurts, the baggage.

After a time, she stood back, and looked at me as if to

say, "Why would you hug me?" and staggered out into the cold. Her father looked at me and nodded...and hobbled out into the cold after her. I don't even know her name.

I went back to the corner where the drums were, but Pastor 'dad' was playing the big one I had been using... The hand drum...I love that one, about the size of a good pizza pie, and it sounds awesome... I danced in the back, beating the drums... When that time was over, we kept on them, beating them, I was dancing. There's something about it all, like marching into a battle, a spiritual battle, a victory. It was for that woman, whatever it was. It was for my other self. It was for my brother. It was for the 14-year-old boy who cried out to Him in anger, for a sign, and received me as such.

It was something I will never forget. A memory I will carry with me always, in my pursuit.

30 November 2005

White Friars, London

Every day I am in awe of the Love and Peace of God. I am bound by some undeniable and unbreakable covenant between my spirit and Christ Jesus, to stay to the course before me no matter what the cost, no matter what the road towards it is or isn't paved with. That covenant goes far beyond my salvation, which has been assured to me by the beautiful, violent sacrifice on the Cross. It was sealed that moment and has been, every second of every day since then become more real and apparent to me.

Daily I am compelled to fall on my knees before an awesome and magnificent King, not in some terrified submission, but out of the deep and fragrant love we share. I anoint Him with the oil of my life, the salty tears of joy I cry as He brings me out of the dark places and closer to the Rainbow around His Throne. With my hair, my only crowning glory, I wash His feet - even when I thought I was dying... and my hair was coming out - and He calls me beautiful. The cost of that oil is unnamed in dollars, euros, pounds, shekels.... I've bought that oil with my life, my pain, joy, sickness, grief, happiness, loss, gain... It is all I have, and daily I give it to Him as others scoff at me. Sound familiar?

I can't recall the exact moment when my Yeshua met me on the street, naked in my sin and shame, all my accusers standing ready to stone me. I was three then, and the years following were filled with stumbling... I had forgotten how He asked me "Woman, where are your accusers?" and still do at times. By His loving kindness He sends the Holy Spirit to remind me those words every day. Each moment of each day I walk closer to the joy of my salvation, always stepping further away from the place of pain and defeat that I once believed was for me - even though Jesus promised me otherwise. And here He is again! Reminding me daily by His faithfulness and long suffering that I AM a radiant bride, living in victory and growing in grace.

HE crowns me with the dignity and beauty that all my enemies would try in vain to dispute. He wakes me every morning and washes my face, no scales over my eyes.... He bathes me in the same water He gave me when I met Him at the well and He loved me in spite of my sins. Gently He washes the stains of the day off my person with the balm of forgiveness and the oil of gladness. He gives me fresh fine robes and doesn't remind me how beautiful the rags were when He first clothed me in them, nor how costly they were, nor how many times He's had to remove my worldly, tattered clothes and begin again from my freshly bathed nakedness. He never scoffs at me for losing the fine gems He gives me... only giving me more when I understand how I lost them.

Every day I feel the kisses on my cheek, face.... the Spirit of God reminding me that I am loved. I am pulled to that Love and its sweet purity. I long to give it on this earth and receive it in kind. Holy Spirit shows me the love stored up within myself as I go through my day, learning faith from Mom, teachability from my students, forgiveness from my children, calmness from Ofir.... He shows Himself to me in everyone I meet and everything I do and see, and grows my compassion, justice and kindness through them.

When my days are ended and I am lying in my little bed next to Him, I thank Him for all those people and the ways they bless me... and still longing for the one He's promised me to find me... I fall asleep held close to the heart of my Lover. Someday He will hold both of us there, my true love and me, and I will love him as I love my Jesus - with everything I am.

My desire is for purity and intimacy with the Father, Son and Holy Spirit. Above all else if I am remembered for anything in my life, I long to be remembered as a woman who loved God, and knew her Lover, Jesus and walked with the Spirit of God. I long to be remembered as a mystic who defied man and religion and sat at the foot of the Throne of Grace, leaned on the Breast of my Savior, and lived in and with and through Holy Spirit. Not as a prophetess who prayed over nations, or as a wonderful mentor or worship singer - all that is fleeting, I want Him and Him alone. When the day is ended,

I hope I have loved and uplifted rather than torn down and judged.

Daily I fail and daily I achieve that goal, but my Jesus is pleased when I have tried and learned and come as far as He set out for me.

This is my walk as an everyday Christian. Perhaps this seems a little extreme to people, but my Lover, my Jesus is an extreme Jesus who doesn't follow the rules of the world or try to please man. My God and Father is the King of the Universe, a Mighty Warrior who defends His own, and isn't looking for me to be a militant twit for Christ. His Spirit is in me and around me at all times and it is His eyes I choose to see this world through.... My chosen path is in service to Him, Them and I love it. Perhaps I am an exception to the rules of man, and for that I am happy. Every day I strive to break those rules and walk and live in the Spirit of Love which is Christ. Here is the reason for my joy and hope, my peace and strength.

Daily the old me is dying, a slow painful, screaming death at times, nonetheless dying. Always dying so that I might become a better mother, wife, friend, sister, daughter.... Always dying so that I might be closer to the Living God, dwelling in the Beauty Realm of His presence, beholding the glory of Heaven in this life and eternally.

h.e. newell

13 October 2005
London
Darling....

London was beautiful today; I so wish you were here. I went very early this morning with Jael on the bus to school and enjoyed that time with her greatly. Although, I think it's getting easier to say goodbye to her in the morning, I am always happy when she comes home after school. I like my girls to be home with me.

The trains were quiet this morning as I went down to CL. On one train I stood by the door between cars and my hair got caught up in the draft... It felt so good, like being back by the sea again - I miss the sea. Memories of wishing you were with me on the beach came back to me then...and stayed with me all day long. Even now as I write this I wonder if we'll ever get to go to the beach and be lazy in love ever. You cannot know how much I would love that - or perhaps you do... Who can know what's coming?

St Paul's Cathedral was my stop, but I had purposed in my mind to go to St Sepulchre to see where my ancestor lived and died so many years ago. There was so much peace there, it was amazing, and I wondered then if you felt it also. I pictured you there with me, enjoying those moments and I wondered if you would have enjoyed them for what they were - moments of beauty - or because you enjoyed seeing my delight there.

It's almost too much for me to tell you the rest of my day. My heart is aching, and I am longing for you. There's not an erotic sort of yearning, it's not lust. Some love transcends those things and meets you in a place that is so deep it completes you just because your heart is part of another person. This is the longing I have for you. I feel very empty without you... And yet, sometimes in your absence I feel as though you are right here beside me, holding me, kissing my head at night, looking into my eyes and knowing me, saying my name against my ear and smiling when it gives me a shiver... Everything earthly that I am is yours, and everything God will allow me to share with you... is yours. It's all I have to give you, I'm afraid.

I'm writing to you for years now, I hope soon you'll come to me. Sometimes I feel as though I will meet you today, others it seems like you'll never find me. Have I met you? Do you see me when you close your eyes at night? Are you alone? Lonely? Longing like me? Do you write to me? Do you long for these letters I've been writing you? Today I wondered if you would be as smitten with me when you finally find me as I am with you before you have.

This last year without you has been so hard. I've wanted so much to live life with deliberate joy... but I feel as though I failed in some ways; as though all my joy was painted on... I'm wanting so much to laugh out loud and sing and dance on the beach with you... Please find me soon so that telling you about my day doesn't leave me feeling so empty inside.

Always yours,
Yours

(taken from my notebook: 2 august 2005, 8ish pm)

So, I am at St Alban's in a doorway on the old arch of the monastery built in 1311 or something like that. All around me I feel the presence of God. His sweet and gentle presence. I've had to take some time out, a moment to sit and reflect on all that is in my spirit lately... There is some great awakening going on in me, as though all the sorrow of my years is falling to the ground. And where can I go that His Love won't restore the losses I have felt in my heart these many years?

In some way it's very much as though I have been martyred to this world and sacrificed on His altar for a greater thing in His mind. A life of purpose and sanctification requires it, doesn't it?

So. I am here at this ancient place of worship, wondering what the spirit of God is pouring into me. And all around me I feel the cloud of witnesses; I can hear their psalms and prayers - their intimate and beautiful moments with the Bridegroom... How sweet... how precious... how lovely it must be to Him.

The sun is setting, and I can hear a piper in the distance. The question is: the piper... is he sent for me?

The bells of St Alban's are sounding - calling - and there's peace like a river here. I want to wander back through the church yard and rest again by a long-passed bishop of Newcastle... His marker vibrated with the anointing when I touched it... He must have been so close to the Lord! When I am gone on, will my legacy be one of purpose and intimacy? Will my prayers be heard alongside the bells and whispers of the witnesses gone on before me? Will my life have exemplified the sweet and pure love that heals others?

I would love to share this moment with my other self. And I pray that while I enjoy these beautiful moments, he will also feel the peace and love that I am receiving now. If he were here, I would look deep into his eyes and smile just for him, seeing myself when I looked there. I would hold him close to my heart and imprint the moment forever. My prince and I... :)

The sun is setting... the cathedral here reminds me of the western wall. It looks like gold. Jesus always gives the best... these moments are treasures now, gold... My spirit is full of joy and peace. My heart is overflowing like some cup of the best wine... my sweetheart, Jesus, this moment... my girls finding small treasures in the grass...

a perfect sunset...

Prophetic words

Palanquin
August 2004

I saw the Bride being carried in a palanquin. Mighty warrior angels on all corners, making certain nothing in heaven or on earth could stop the Bride from reaching her Beloved. Around the palanquin was a vast army of cherubim and warrior angels. They said in a loud, wonderful chorus: "here is the Bride of the Son of Man! Make a sure path all you princes and principalities, for the Bride is coming to the bedchamber!"

The palanquin was adorned with gems, all the colors of the 12 gems of the ephod. Each gem seemed to sing a different song, relay a different thanksgiving hymn. The poles were golden, and strong, making certain nothing touched the Bride or her litter. The veil protecting the bride was white gauzy linen, woven with gold, so that none could look on her before she met her Bridegroom.

I watched this palanquin with its mighty host pass through vineyards, and young girls cried out: "Here is the Bride of the Son of the Most High God! We well press new wine for their honor!" They tossed grape leaves in the air and celebrated the passing of the Bride through the vineyards.

When the palanquin reached the chambers, the Bridegroom stepped out, and parted the veils. His light was so powerful and pure, the Bride was completely hidden from view. He walked her to the chamber and all the host of Heaven began to sing: "At last the Bride is home with her Beloved! At last, the Heavens rejoice!"

I saw the Lord smile and say "It is pleasing to have the Bride in my house with my Son. What I have put together, let no man take apart"

When I asked the Holy Spirit about these mysteries, He said: "The time of intimacy is here. I am moving the people of God into a level of intimacy that can only be from on High. There will be tears and joy, breaking and healing, and they will know the heart of the Most High God! They will know His heart is for them, and they will be undone. I am pouring out the peace, and the love of the Father, I am breaking hearts for the Lost as my people come into new intimacy with Him."
"This season, I am making it clear, what is religion and what is relationship, and the Bride will sing out loudly, "My beloved has a relationship with me!" A new

freedom in worship will come, a new communion, when my bride enters into a deeper intimacy with me, with the Lord Most High."

I saw the Bride come out of the chambers, beautiful and round with love. Pregnant and ready to give birth. The Spirit said to me, "Bring forth a new intimacy, Daughter of Zion! Call forth the nations into the embrace of the Father! Birth healing through your groanings, and joy through your praise. Daughter of Zion, dance on the back of the enemy, take back hearts and land and show them to the palanquin waiting just for them."

5:53am
7 August 2004

I woke up this morning leaping out of my bed with great expectation that has been in me for some days now. I asked the Lord about this vision I had last night, and all about the bride chambers. This is what the Lord spoke to me:

"I am taking my people through a time of purification. Get ready for a setting aside time. This time of preparation comes before the palanquin is sent to carry the Bride. There must be a cleansing, stripping, wearing off of the old self, so that only the virginal purity remains.

"Just like Hadassah preparing, I am taking the Bride through a season of preparation. Preparation for the night you will spend with the King. There was a selection process, and now the consecration. Cleansing and scrubbing, "dietary" cleansing, and deep perfuming. There are new robes and fine adornments for you that I cannot place upon a filthy body. Sometimes the cleansing may burn and be uncomfortable. Sometimes the "food" will make you vomit out all that is impure in your belly. Sometimes the humility of your nakedness as I strip away the rags will leave you feeling vulnerable. Sweet perfume will be so fragrant you will forget every foul stench you've ever known. Even the overwhelming beauty of your new robes will bring you to tears.

He Prepares a Table for Me 123

There is coming the hour, when I am making my Bride a warrior Bride. A Queen must be prepared to battle alongside her King. And the Bride will be so strong and ready, she will be able to go into battle in her pregnant state. This is why there is so much preparation."

I saw the Lord holding the Bride in His arms as He made her bare of all the rags (shame) she clung to. She leaned into Him and cried until His robes were soaked from breast to floor. He covered her nakedness, with a tremendous light, and her vulnerability was His alone. In a breath He anointed her to her very spirit, and the fragrance filled the room. Even the hosts of Heaven began to rejoice and at it filling the air. With a piece of His robes, He dressed her. The linen was the purest white I've ever seen. It covered her bareness, which was now clothed in splendor.

When He laid her to rest on a bed of pillows and silk, He said to me, "Daughter come and see, here is all i have for this child." I came with Him to a room full of coffers, armor golden and strong... There were war banners and Jewels, and He called this room "ta ruach muzav" (golden spirit cell), saying it was her place only.

When she woke up, He showed me a room with a table and three chairs. He said, "Now we eat with the Bride, she needs good fruit." We sat a while, and while she ate, he fed her from His plate, the choicest pieces. She ate like a child hungry after a famine, and He patiently fed her until she was full for a moment.

He looked across the table to me and said, "Daughter of Zion, bring the rest to me, so I can make them ready." With this He kissed my head and warm sweet oil poured out on me. My hair became sticky and dripped as I went out from there.

"This is the season" says the Spirit of the Lord, "For the mature to bring in the immature, for the loved to bring in the unloved. Those who bring the Bride to the King must be consecrated themselves. Bring yourself into a time of preparation and sacrifice before the Lord!"

8 January 2005

The Lord says, "Decree a thing and make it so. All the promises I have made are good and just, faithful to come to pass, but you must declare it so. Decree a thing and give it life, just as I breathed the very life that is in you. Speak the word and let it be so. I have given you creative power for you are made in my own image.

"Decree a thing; proclaim the promises and you will see fruit. Post the declarations on the gates of the enemy. Sound the trumpet in the city walls; announce that the day of grace is upon you. The days of Grace are here. In the day fresh rain will fall, by night the flowers and plants drink in all the nutrition. Before you know it, the harvest comes even though you did not see the germination of every single seed; you trust that I have made it grow.

"Can any man be behind the scenes of his own life? Surely not. But I, the Lord your God have been everywhere, even the dark places. I have worked through things you thought impossible because you could not see. I have germinated seeds you have thought dead because you did not see me working in your chosen season.

"Here is the season of reaping. The promises and decrees will come to pass, the seeds will come to fruit. If you have seen me as unfaithful, surely that day is passed. How can the sun be unfaithful simply because it does not push the clouds aside? How can the Lord be unfaithful simply because my timing differs from yours? I have seen grounds soaked with weeping, I have seen breasts bruised with beating, I have heard the cries of my people and I have moved. Who can know my ways? Who can know my mind? Who can foresee my actions unless I speak to them?

"Decree a thing," says the Lord. "Make your declarations heard. How can you say that you are children of promise if you do not know what the promises are? Ask me, and I will show you. Seek me and I will find you. Listen and I will tell you all I have promised to you. Decree a thing. Reach deep into your heart and find me. Reach deep into your spirit and find me. Wait and recall all I have promised you and decree it. Give it life. Give it authority.

"Take My signet and make your decrees. Seal the scrolls and know that they are written with Kingly authority.

"How many of you are standing for my Holy city? The city David gave to me. The city which rejected my Grace, the city I weep for? Blessed are those who stand for my Holy City, who weep for the lambs of Israel. The blessings of Jacob are upon those whose hearts are torn for Israel. The peace of Shiloh is upon those who weep for my chosen nation. Decree a thing over the children of Israel and set them free. Speak life into the sons of Zion and share my Joy.

"How will you use the authority I have given you? How will you use my signet? I will open up the heavenlies for the one who will use it wisely, the one who will use it as I would. Watch and see what I have done on your behalf. Watch and see the works of the Lord. Open your eyes and see the fruit of all your weeping and sowing. Broaden your scope and see what the Lord will have you do in His name."

128   h.e. newell

26/27 January 2006

Look. Watch and see what I am about to do. The cold wind from the North brings change. I am coming from the North like a mighty hurricane across the Land. I am bringing change. I am breathing across the Land in a new way, and no one will be able to miss it. I am coming from the North, doing a new thing and I am not holding back My Glory.

Watch and see what I am about to do. I am setting the North on Fire. I am setting the wheels in motion for a mighty and terrible display of My Power. I will shine across the North like the Northern Lights have never done. I will redeem what has been stolen from the North and I will cause them to be the envy of many nations. I will heal the Land; I will restore the wealth of the peoples who were stripped bare. I am setting up my Holy Habitation in the North and I will spread my Glory out across the Land from there like the magnificent train of My robes.

I am King over the North.

*I am coming to Finland. She waits for me like a girl on the platform waits for the return of her lover. I am over Finland now, brooding, waiting, watching, listening. This is My Land; these are My people. I have watched for far too long as My people have been overlooked and left out. I have watched My people live under the judgements and pride of other nations, and I am acting now. The first shall be last and the last shall be first. Those who wait on Me shall be blessed. I am about to do a thing in Helsinki that no one has ever seen before. I have heard the cries of my people there and I am answering. Like a mighty tidal wave of fire, I will take back My city. I will restore the joy and beauty of the city and the hope of the people. I will perform miracles signs and wonders even in the streets, and the world will take notice of the city that I love.

I am brooding over Lapland. I am bringing My remnant people there into their kingship. I am burning off the ropes of bitterness and breaking the chains of slavery and poverty among my remnant there. I am going to show the world how much I love this people and cause them to see how beautiful and esteemed they are in my sight. I AM the God of Lapland, I AM the Shining One, and I will rest over the Land of the Midnight Sun.

I am coming from the North, like a mighty rushing flood. I am bathing Finland in My Glory. I will bring nations to their knees; they will say that Finland has been wronged and ask forgiveness. They will say that Finland is a beautiful land, they will say that Finns are my people, and they will speak blessings and cease the cursing. Finland shall be the head and not the tail, and she shall wear the crown of righteousness. People from every nation will know the name 'Finland' when I am finished, when I have made my display there. The blood in the Land has cried out for vengeance and I have heard. I am bringing a new sort of peace between the nations and Finland. The blood in the Land will cease crying.

There is coming a time when witches will repent and turn their faces to the Spirit of God. They will see the Bridegroom and tremble and repent. They will fall dead where they stand as they try to hold back My Hand. I am redeeming the prophets and apostles I have set in Finland. I will give them a choice to serve Me or die. When My Fire falls in the Land, they will know the truth and make a choice. I am healing and restoring families in Finland. Fathers must be fathers, husbands must be husbands, and when My fire overtakes the Land, they will turn their hearts to Me and return. Wives and husbands will live according to My plan.

I am restoring hope and joy. I am removing the darkness. I am removing the veil from the eyes of the people for a time. They will choose Me or perish. They will worship me in the fullness of the Spirit, and they will be known throughout the Land as a people who love their God.*

Watch and see what I do when I come and make my Name known throughout the North. Watch and see the Glory of my Name overtake the Land. I AM the star

He Prepares a Table for Me 131

in the North, and I will not share My Glory. I will not share my praise. I am a jealous God, and I will not share my lover Finland. I have claimed her, and she is Mine. I will protect her like a warrior drunk with wine.

Who can dare to think that I will share my Glory! Watch and see what I do! The first shall be least and the last shall be first.

*I am about to do a mighty thing in Siberia. Salt. Salt of the earth. I am about to bring the salt to the people. I am bringing justice to the people. I am extending My Hand over the Land. I am the Lord over Siberia, and I have watched for too long as my people suffered there. I am bringing my Fire there. I dare men to try to keep My Fire out of the Land. I am bringing the Glory of my presence to Siberia. The blood in the ground is crying out to me. Day and night the ground is seeking Justice. I have called Siberia mine, and I am dispatching warring angels to drive out the prince over the land. The oppressors will be brought to Justice and my people there will praise My Name in the streets.

I will restore all the gold stolen by the few over the centuries, the dignity, the hope, the freedom. I am bringing a liberty to the Land that has never been seen there before. I am bringing boldness and joy back to the people. I am restoring the riches of the Land to the people. I am coming from the North, and I will show the people signs and miracles. I am bringing the rainbow of my presence to the Land. I am settling over the Land like a sweet fragrance. I will show them I am there by signs in the sky, signs in the weather, miraculous happenings, and they will know that I am their God and I have not forgotten them.

I am about to humble the proud. I am about to slap the hands of the oppressors. No longer will they take food from the mouths of babies. There will be a new revolution in the Land: My revolution, and nothing they do will stop it. For every martyr they have made I am raising up 10 more believers. For every mouth they have silenced I am opening 10 more. I will make it impossible for them to subdue this revolution. The harder they fight it the more mouths I will open. The eyes of the world will be upon the nation, and they will be unable to deceive any longer. *

Watch and see what I do. Watch and see how a Good Father keeps His promises. Look into the cloud of witnesses and see how I am answering prayers. Who can know my timing? And who can judge it?

*I am making restorations in Yugoslavia. Croatia, Serbia, Bosnia, brothers. I am restoring the beauty and dignity of the land. I am bringing brothers together. I am bringing a Godly repentance among the people there. Brothers apologising to brothers. My Glory poured out over the Land. I gave my people a beautiful and prosperous land, I and the Land has cried out to me: "Father Creator, how long do we have to taste the bitterness of the selfishness of brothers?" The Land is like a traumatized child, the people are survivors of a waking nightmare. I want to restore the purity of their minds. I want to heal the devastation of Land and Man in Yugoslavia. I am about to erase the imprints of destruction in the minds and spirits of my people there. I am breaking down the walls there and reuniting my people. I am sending signs and wonders to the Muslims there. I am reviving the church there. Sleepers awake!!

There is a wind coming from the North. The wind of My Spirit coming like a great turbulence. I am sending fresh rain to wash the ground clean; I am sending the wind to blow away the dust. I am sending fire to burn off the dross in the Land; in waves of Fire, I am going to move over the Land. What was once divided I am declaring, I am commanding to reunite. The whole of the Land will be unable to deny the might of My Hand. Brothers and sisters worshipping the King of the Universe together. Every nation will look and say: "Look what God has done in Yugoslavia! He has done what seemed impossible!" *
Watch and see what I do. Watch and see how I will do these things to preserve my Holy Name. For the sake of My Holy Name, I will not withhold My power. My blessings, my mercy, my justice, I will share in abundance.

In the next six months I am relocating, repositioning, reassigning, realigning. I am moving pieces into place; I am setting up the stage for what is coming. In the next six months I am preparing my Bride for a great work. I am going to test my people. I am going to elevate those who have been waiting in the background, I am going to move those who are in the spotlight to the background. I will not share My Glory. Men will no longer be able to tell Me who is fit to minister, who is worthy of blessing, who is prepared. I AM raising up Joshuas, Jehus, Elishas, Peters, Lydias, Deborahs, Esthers in this hour. Who can dare to question my choices now?

I am rearranging the structure on the church; I am moving people out of their comfort zones. I will not use the unwilling, and I will not beg. I will not ask repeatedly while willing servants wait for a commission. I will send and they will go, or they will be left out of what I am about to do. I am no longer protecting the ones who habitually sin and shame My Holy Name. I am no longer holding back the enemy from his legal claims to harass such people. My mercy and justice are mine to give and withhold. I am no longer tolerating drowsiness or deception in My Camp. I am no longer tolerating bitterness and division, pride and false humility and holiness. I have served warnings time after time, now I am serving notice. In the next six months I am going to sift the tares and the wheat. I will cover the humble, I will bless the meek and I will send out the submissive and willing.

In the next six months I am revealing strategies to the few who will work with me not for themselves. I will show them my plans, I will show them where and when and how. I will show them who and why and for how long. I will make divine connections, I will set up meetings, I will teach and train my people I will give them stamina for the coming work. Those who work of their own strength will fall and I will leave them in their folly.

How long have I shown mercy? How long have I held back the accuser? On a Word he will delight in harassing the ones who have tested my patience and tried my temper. I am saying the word to him right now. I am giving him permission to harass and press my people. When they give him legal rights to interfere, I will not hold him back any longer. In the next six months they will cry out to Me: where are You, Lord?" yet I will not answer. In the next six months they will say to Me: "Forgive us Lord!" but I will know their hearts and hear the emptiness of their apology and I will not answer. I am weary of lip service. I am not a God who will be mocked with empty words and false worship. I will not be insulted by prideful men who think that I am a blind and foolish God.

In the next six months I am exposing false leaders. I am revealing witchcraft in the church and in the governments. I will expose corruption and theft in the finances of households, churches, nations, cities. I will bring judgements on the rulers who have abused power. I will bring justice to the senates and counsels who have been overruled and vetoed when they have tried to uphold just laws. I will bless and preserve righteous men who have fought to preserve human life, dignity and Godly justice in their lands. I will shield them from accusations, scandals and attacks, because they have loved Me and My Law and stood up for it. I will no longer hold back the enemy from the unjust. Though they seem to prosper and flourish in spite of their pride and deceitfulness, I will expose them. Though the people may continue to choose them over righteous men, I will reject them.

I am exposing witchcraft in the body of Christ. I am judging rebelliousness and manipulation, sorcery and divination for what it is: witchcraft and idolatry. No man can serve two masters. No man who understands this principle of who I AM can continue to do so and not fear retribution. I will reveal to my people the rebellion in them, and I will hold them accountable to repent. I will judge the unteachable and the prideful when they choose to keep their ways and not to surrender to mine. The time is coming when I will accept nothing but a total surrender in my anointed servants: prophets, apostles, teachers, evangelists, pastors. The time is coming when I will strike down the self-appointed. Only My Son appoints the few who are chosen before the universe was breathed into being, and I will not tolerate man assuming the authority of Christ.

In the next six months I will send signs and wonders through the weather. I will send more natural disasters to judge the nations for their actions, verdicts and passiveness. I will send blessings to the oppressed, and warnings to the oppressors. I will make it known that I am a God of Justice and Vengeance. I will have mercy on whom I will have mercy, and I will withhold it when I withhold it. Who can tell the God of the Universe how to judge? Who can tell the Creator how to rule His creation?

Here is what I am going to do: I will listen from My Holy places as my Name is extolled from every corner of the earth. Even as men harden their hearts, those who love me will become louder and bolder.

*I am looking at the United Kingdom. I am looking at England now. In England I am about to change the church. I am going to change the government. I am going to expose the lies and the laziness that have been kept from the people. I am going to restore sovereignty to the throne in England and place a God-fearing man on it. I will transfer the authority and power to the next generation. I am raising up a righteous, conscientious, able and strong leader in the next generation - he will be the rightful ruler. He will govern with justice and kindness. I will place the mantle of the ages over him and protect him.

I am removing the façade from the people and showing them truth. I am going to wake the sleepers. I will expose the curses on the land and the intercessors will pray blessings where the curses have been. I will send the angel armies to drive out the princes in the land for a season. I will give the church an open heaven for a season and see what they do with it. I will open the heavens over the entire UK and see what the church does. Will they repent? Will they praise Me? Will they partake of the blessings? Will they unite? I will open the heavens over all of Ireland, Wales, Scotland, and England and give the church an open window to call down a revival. I will see if they are desperate enough to see Me glorified in the Land.

I will have unity in the church if not in the land. I will have unity in the church if not in the government, or I will close the heavens and move on. I have called the United Kingdom to be a Holy Land, and I will not share my Glory. I have called the United Kingdom to be a doorway between west and east, and I will see my people safely come through there. I have given the United Kingdom wealth, and now I will see it shared. *
Even now I am coming from the North and I am bringing change. Even now I am lining things up as I will have them aligned. Who can challenge the mind of God? Who can criticise my ways and means? I know what I am doing. I knew what I was doing before the

Universe took shape. I will do what I please, and I will not be challenged. I will not bless a church that challenges me. I will not bless a people who mock me. I will not bless a church who thinks I can be deceived with actions and hollow words.

*Watch what I do in France. Watch how I set Paris ablaze with My wondrous love. Watch how I bring justice to France. Breaking down every stronghold, I will be the first love in the Land. Who is going to France to pray? Who is crying out for the Land? Who is going to pray in the streets? Who is walking the corridors of her palaces and praying? Who is stirring up old wells in her monasteries? Watch what I will do if even one person cries out to me for France.

Even now I am coming from the North. I am coming to drive out the perversion in the Land. I am coming to redeem the blood in the ground which cries out for vengeance. I am bringing restoration to a devastated Land. Even now I am returning France to her former glory. Who will cry out on behalf of the people there?

Watch what I do in France. Watch the romance unfold between Me and France. Watch the people declare My Holiness, My faithfulness, My Sovereignty. Watch Me pour out my Spirit there and bring a hunger for more to the starving people there. Watch me break the curses spoken so many centuries over the people and elevate them before all the world. Watch and see what

I do. Watch and see. Watch as people take notice of what I can do. Watch as people begin to realise that there is a God in Heaven who loves France. Watch as the Fire of My Holiness spreads through the Land like no one has ever seen. *

March 2010

During a conversation I was having with the Lord today about the health-care bill, and what it means for the people... the Lord gave me this Word:

"Wouldn't it confound the world if God's people had no need for a health-care reform? Why are you up in arms about this health-care bill passing? Haven't I promised to take care of you? Haven't I shown you that healing is the children's bread? Haven't I given over my own Son to be whipped and torn to purchase every healing for you? Haven't I given you all authority over sickness and iniquity in the Name of my Son Jesus Christ? Haven't you been promised that you would see and do even greater works in your season?

"I have a greater health care plan for my people than any government could ever impose upon you.

"Have you forgotten?

"I am releasing the healing virtue. I am pouring it out like never before. But I am imparting it to those who would have the boldness to call on it no matter where; no matter who; no matter what.

"This is the season where I will test who fully relies on Me; who fully trusts the Living God - the God who heals; who truly receives the priestly authority and kinship I have offered them. This is the season where I am separating the wheat and the tares.

"I want you to depend on Me, but I am giving you a

choice: Live in discontent, depending on men whose hearts are sinister by nature; or live in victory and be content as you draw from MY economy. I have only your needs in My heart.

"Let me 'worry' about those in power who do not act according to what glorifies Me. Your part is to live a life of faith and prayer, walking in intimacy with Me and holiness. Pray that the hearts of the people would turn to Me and receive My Son and the Salvation that comes only through Him.

"Keep your eyes on Me and not on what's happening all around you. This way you will be able to focus on loving the lost into a place of Grace, sharing the Hope you have with them, presenting them to My Son as a new Bride.

"Begin in your own lives and watch lives around you transform."

The Lord showed me this prayer directive: Repent and come out of unholy covenants; agreements with the enemy regarding health, identity, financial situations etc. IE; accepting a diagnosis as the final word; saying "I have (OCD, Diabetes... etc.)" or owning illnesses; "my (arthritis, asthma, cancer etc) God did not create illness (or poverty), and He does not give it to us.

(1) Do not accept or agree with these things, give them back to Satan and be free. Reject and step out of defeatist thinking.

"I will always be an addict"

"If God wants to heal me."

"This is God's way of keeping me dependent upon Him."

Jesus suffered so that we could not only be saved, but that we would be new creations (2), and that we would live a healthy abundant life. He WANTS to heal and bless us. Receive and declare that you are a child of God, that healing is the children's bread (3) and that by His stripes we are healed (4). Remember Jesus' sacrifice and victory by taking communion every day (5). Tell at least one person per day about the Lord and something He has done for you (6). Remain in this place of fellowship with the Holy Spirit and victory by reciting or meditating on scriptures that recall the faithful nature of our God (7). (1) Job 1: 12 "All right, you may test him," the Lord said to Satan. "Do whatever you want with everything he possesses, but don't harm him physically." So, Satan left the Lord's presence. 2 Corinthians 5:17 This means that anyone who belongs to Christ has become a new person. The old life is gone; a new life has begun! (3) Matt 15:22-28 (4) Isaiah 53:5 5 But he was pierced for our rebellion, crushed for our sins. He was beaten so we could be whole. He was whipped so we could be healed. (5) Luke 22: 19 He took some bread and gave thanks to God for it. Then he broke it in pieces and gave it to the disciples, saying, "This is my body, which is given for you. Do this to remember me." (6) Revelation 12:11 And they have defeated him by the blood of the Lamb and by their testimony. And they did not love their lives so much that they were afraid to die. (7)

2 Thessalonians 3:3 (TLV)
But the Lord is trustworthy—and He will strengthen and protect you from the evil one.

Selah!

The Word of the Lord is eternal. It is complete. Whether it is poetry or Scripture, He has the final say. Treasure every sacred word. Celebrate them all at your banquet!

Isaiah 22:22 (TLV)
I will set the key[a] of the house of David upon his shoulder—what he opens, no one can shut; what he shuts, and no one can open.

Revelation 3:7 (TLV)
To the angel of Messiah's community in Philadelphia write: "Thus says the Holy One, the True One, who has the key of David, who opens and no one will shut, and who shuts and no one opens:

h.e. newell

Thoughts...

About the author

What can I say about myself?

If I am remembered for nothing else in this life, my hope is that people will hear my name and remember that I was a mystic. That I was fully and truly consumed with the desire to know and understand the Heart of God. Thank you for drinking from the deep wells of the Lord with me. I'll share more with you soon!
throneroomjewel@gmail.com

Made in the USA
Middletown, DE
18 January 2022